WORKBOOK

FOR

Practicing The Way

Be With Jesus. Become Like Him. Do As He Did.

An Implementation Guide to John Mark Comer's Book

SAGE READS

DISCLAIMER:

This book is an independently published and UNOFFICIAL workbook for "Practicing the Way." It is not affiliated, endorsed, or sanctioned by the original book's author or publisher.

The intention of creating this workbook is not to mislead you, but rather to offer genuine assistance in complementing and enhancing your understanding of the main book. This workbook is intended to be used alongside the original book, not as a substitute for it.

This BOOK Belongs To

Exclusive Bonus!

As a token of our appreciation, we are delighted to offer you complimentary access to three workbooks featuring some of the best-selling books in the US. To access these books, simply scan the QR code below. This will direct you to a secure link where you can download the workbooks for free.

We believe these additional workbooks will complement your learning journey and provide further insights into impactful literature.

Should you have any questions, feedback, or if you're interested in exploring special deals or collaborations, feel free to reach out to us via our email at sagereads1@gmail.com.

Table of Contents

How to Use This Workbook

Welcome to this extensive workbook for "Practicing the Way," crafted to enhance your engagement with and practical application of the lessons and ideas from the book. This workbook has been carefully created to accompany you on your spiritual journey, offering a structured and interactive experience to cultivate a more intentional and discipleship-focused life.

1. **Understanding the purpose:** Begin by grasping the purpose of this workbook, which is to guide you through a process of self-reflection and personal growth. Recognize that the information provided is intended to help you delve deeper into various aspects of your life and spiritual direction.
2. **Engaging with the Content:** Explore the modules, covering a variety of topics such as decision-making, spiritual journey, hospitality, service, and discipleship. Take your time reading through each module, paying close attention to the insights and prompts provided.
3. **Self-Reflective Questions:** Take note of the self-reflective questions provided in each module. These questions are designed to prompt introspection and encourage you to examine different facets of your life, beliefs, and behaviors. Consider each question meticulously and take the time to journal or contemplate your responses.
4. **Action Prompts:** Take note of the action prompts or implementation activities provided alongside the self-reflective questions. These prompts provide useful strategies for applying the insights gained from self-

reflection to your daily life. Consider how you may integrate these activities into your routines and habits.

5. **Create your plan:** Based on your responses to the self-reflective questions and the action prompts, develop a personalized plan for growth and improvement. Identify particular areas of your life where you want to see change or improvement, then devise tangible means to achieving it.
6. **Implementing Changes:** Put your plan into action by integrating the suggested activities and practices into your daily life. Be deliberate in implementing these changes into your routines and habits, and track your progress over time.
7. **Regular Review and Adjustment:** Regularly review your progress and reflect on any changes or improvements you have experienced. Be open to adjusting your plan as needed based on new insights or circumstances that may arise along the way.
8. **Seeking Support:** Don't hesitate to seek support from trusted friends, mentors, or spiritual advisors as you work through this workbook. Sharing your experience with others could provide valuable accountability, encouragement, and insight.
9. **Celebrating Growth:** Finally, celebrate your growth and accomplishments along the way. Recognize the progress you have made and the positive changes you have implemented in your life. Use this momentum to continue moving forward on your quest for self-discovery and personal development.

Introduction

This workbook has been carefully curated to lead you on a transformative journey of self-reflection, personal growth, and spiritual development. In the contents of this book, you will embark on an extensive study of multiple facets of your life, beliefs, and values, drawing insights from conversations on topics ranging from decision-making to discipleship.

Life is a journey filled with opportunities for growth and self-discovery. Yet, in the midst of the hustle and bustle of our daily lives, it's easy to lose sight of our innermost desires and aspirations. This workbook acts as a compass, guiding you through the complexities of your journey and revealing the route that resonates with your true self.

Drawing from insightful conversations on topics like surrender, sacrifice, hospitality, and spiritual formation, each module offers a unique perspective on exploring different facets of life and spiritual journey. Through self-reflective questions and actionable prompts, you'll gain more clarity into who you are and where you want to go.

As you engage with the content, you'll be encouraged to reflect on your past experiences, assess your present circumstances, and envision your future aspirations. Each module is accompanied by prompts designed to translate your insights into tangible steps forward, empowering you to take action toward realizing your goals.

Approach this workbook with an open mind and a willingness to embrace vulnerability. While self-reflection can be challenging, it's through facing our fears and doubts that we grow and evolve as individuals. Seek support from trusted friends, mentors, or spiritual advisors as you navigate this journey.

Ultimately, the goal of this workbook is to empower you to live a more authentic, purposeful, and fulfilling life. May it serve as a guiding light, illuminating the path ahead and inspiring you to embrace the fullness of who you are meant to be.

Module 1: Understanding Apprenticeship to Jesus

Reflecting on Your Spiritual Journey

"Reflecting on Your Spiritual Journey" urges you to take a deep, personal examination of your beliefs and spiritual progress. This reflective practice is more than simply a retrospective exercise; it is a transforming process that addresses the past, present, and future of your spiritual life.

The spiritual journey in the Christian context is often viewed as a route of apprenticeship to Jesus. This route is not linear, but rather a dynamic and expanding process characterized by moments of revelation, doubt, learning, and progress. Reflecting on this journey entails looking back at these pivotal moments and determining how they shaped your beliefs and character.

The process starts with remembering. This involves reflecting on major life events - moments of joy, sadness, struggle, and success - and understanding how these experiences impacted your spiritual perceptions and practices. It involves reminiscing on your childhood, early encounters with faith, periods of doubt or questioning, and significant spiritual insights or change.

Following this, there is an examination of the present state of your faith. This necessitates honesty and vulnerability, as well as an understanding of your strengths and weaknesses. It's an opportunity to assess your current spiritual disciplines, community involvement, and how these align with Jesus' teachings and example.

This journey also involves looking forward, setting intentions for continued spiritual growth. It is about recognizing areas for purposeful growth, such as expanding your prayer practice, becoming more involved in a spiritual community, or demonstrating service and compassion in everyday encounters. This future-oriented reflection is grounded in hope and the belief that through the Holy Spirit, continual transformation is possible.

Integral to this journey is the understanding that spiritual growth is both personal and communal. Reflecting on your spiritual journey in the light of "Practicing the Way" means recognizing the role of community - mentors, friends, and faith communities - in shaping your spiritual path. It is about accepting that, while the journey is personal, it is not meant to be taken alone.

This reflection is an act of worship and gratitude, recognizing God's presence and work in your life. It's a practice of acknowledging the grace and love that sustains and empowers your journey, even through challenging times. This gratitude shapes how you view your past and approach your future, grounding you in a sense of purpose and direction.

Defining Apprenticeship in Your Own Terms

Apprenticeship in terms of following Jesus is a profound, purposeful commitment to learning from and imitating Him in all aspects of life. This method to discipleship, based on Jesus' teachings and model, provides a transforming route that goes beyond intellectual knowledge or ritualistic practice.

Embracing the role of an apprentice

To be an apprentice of Jesus is to completely immerse yourself in His teachings and embrace His way of life. This is not about a superficial label or a nominal adherence to a set of beliefs but about a profound, life-changing journey of growth and transformation.

Intentional Learning and Practice

Apprenticeship necessitates an active and involved attitude to learning. It is not passive knowledge absorption, but rather actual application, experimentation, and, in certain cases, failure as a means of development. As Jesus' apprentice, you are expected to apply His teachings in real-life situations, learning through both action and reflection.

Relationship and Imitation

Central to the apprenticeship is the relationship with the master. For a Christian, this involves developing a deep, personal connection with Jesus through frequent communication (prayer), reflection on His words (Scripture), and imitation of His behaviors and attitudes. This interaction is at the center of the apprenticeship, guiding and molding the learner's experience.

Transformation and Growth

The ultimate goal of apprenticeship with Jesus is transformation—becoming like Him in thought, speech, and behavior. This transformation is both internal, affecting the heart and mind, and external, influencing actions and interactions with others. It's a holistic change, encompassing every aspect of life.

Community and Accountability

While the apprenticeship experience is personal, it is not meant to be solitary. Engaging with a community of fellow apprentices provides support, encouragement, and accountability. This community exemplifies the body of Christ, with each member contributing to the growth and well-being of others.

Service & Mission

Following Jesus is accepting His purpose in the world. Apprenticeship, therefore, includes serving others and sharing the good news of the kingdom of God. This service is not just an obligation but a natural outflow of the transformation and love experienced in the apprenticeship.

In defining apprenticeship on your own terms, consider these facets as integral components of a lifelong journey with Jesus. It is about continuously learning from Him, becoming more like Him, and carrying out His mission in the world. This apprenticeship is dynamic, changing as you get closer to Jesus and gain a deeper knowledge of His teachings and how they apply to your life and the lives of people around you.

Self-Reflective Questions:

1. How have pivotal moments in my spiritual journey shaped my beliefs and character?

----

2. What childhood experiences or early encounters with faith continue to influence my beliefs today?

3. What are my strengths and weaknesses in terms of spiritual disciplines and community involvement?

4. How can I expand my prayer practice, involvement in a spiritual community, or demonstration of service and compassion?

5. How has my spiritual journey been influenced by mentors, friends, and faith communities?

6. Do I recognize the importance of both personal reflection and communal support in shaping my spiritual path?

7. Do I view every moment and interaction as an opportunity to practice the ways of Jesus?

8. How do I evaluate my unique journey with Jesus, considering my personal experiences, situations, and spiritual gifts?

----

9. Am I committed to implementing Jesus' teachings in a way that is true to my own life and circumstances, fostering a dynamic and transformative spiritual path?

Action Prompts:

- **Journaling and Reflection:**
  Set aside regular time for journaling about past experiences and their impact on your spiritual journey.

- **Honest Self-Assessment:**
  Conduct a thorough self-assessment of your current spiritual practices and involvement in your faith community.

- **Goal Setting:**
  Identify specific areas for growth and set actionable goals for spiritual development.

- **Community Engagement:**
  Seek out opportunities for deeper involvement in your faith community and meaningful connections with mentors and peers.

- **Integrating Faith:**
  Practice mindfulness and intentionality in integrating your faith into daily activities and interactions.

- **Personalized Application of Learning:**
  Actively seek opportunities to apply Jesus' teachings in real-life situations, reflecting on the outcomes and lessons learned.

- **Commitment to Dynamic Growth:**
  Make a purposeful commitment to implement Jesus' teachings in a way that resonates with your own life circumstances, fostering a transformative spiritual journey.

Module 2: Being with Jesus

Establishing a Daily Routine with Jesus

Establishing a daily routine with Jesus involves intentionally structuring your day around practices that draw you closer to Him and align your life with His teachings. This begins by setting up specific times for prayer, Scripture meditation, and reflection, allowing these spiritual disciplines to pervade your daily activities. It's about making time in your busy life to connect with Jesus, striving to comprehend His will and applying His teachings to your interactions, decisions, and responses to life's challenges.

Incorporating Jesus into your everyday routine requires being attentive of His presence in every aspect of your life, including your thoughts, decisions, and actions. This could involve starting your day with a prayer of surrender, inviting Jesus to lead you through the day, or ending your day with a review of where you noticed God's presence and guidance.

A daily routine with Jesus is not just about adding spiritual tasks to your to-do list but about fostering a deeper relationship with Him. It's about allowing the rhythms of prayer, Scripture reading, and other spiritual practices to shape your heart and mind, transforming your inner life and, consequently, your outward actions.

This routine is highly personalized and will differ from person to person. It must be evaluated and adjusted regularly to ensure that it remains a life-giving route to spiritual progress rather than just a list of responsibilities. Establishing such a routine is a continual process of discovering how best to live in communion with Jesus, allowing His life and teachings to inform and transform every aspect of your daily life.

To elaborate on establishing a daily routine with Jesus, we can focus on several key components, each serving as a pillar to build your day around:

Morning Devotion

Start your day with a morning devotion to set a spiritual tone. This can involve prayer, reading a passage from the Bible, and meditating on its application in your life. It's a time to seek guidance, strength, and wisdom for the day ahead.

Reflective Prayer

Incorporate moments of reflective prayer throughout your day. These are opportunities to pause, recenter your thoughts on Jesus, and offer up any challenges or gratitude you are experiencing. It's also a moment to listen and be receptive to what God might be communicating to you.

Scripture Meditation

Dedicate time for deeper meditation on Scripture. This goes beyond reading; it's about engaging with the text, understanding its context, and pondering its meaning in your life. Scripture meditation can provide insights and guidance, shaping your actions and decisions.

Evening Review

End your day with an evening review. Reflect on the day's events, your responses to them, and how you saw God at work. This can be a time of thanksgiving, confession, and contemplation on what adjustments might be needed in your spiritual walk.

Weekly Community Worship

Engage in weekly community worship, whether through a church service, small group meeting, or another gathering of believers. This communal aspect reinforces your daily routine, providing support, accountability, and fellowship.

By weaving these practices into the fabric of your daily life, you create a rhythm that keeps you connected with Jesus, fosters spiritual growth, and equips you to live out your faith authentically in the world.

Creating Your "Secret Place"

As outlined in "Practicing the Way", creating your "Secret Place" is a critical concept in advancing your spiritual journey with God. This space is both literal and metaphorical, providing a dedicated setting for intimate communication and connection with God, free from the distractions and noise of daily life.

The Essence of "Secret Place"

The "Secret Place" is based on Jesus' teachings on prayer, stressing not just the act of praying but also the significance of where it unfolds. Jesus advises retreating to a private room, a "tameion" in Greek, which signifies an inner room or space like a closet or pantry used for solitude and uninterrupted prayer. This concept indicates the importance of solitude, silence, and stillness in cultivating a spiritual life.

Personalizing Your Sacred Space

The "Secret Place" is deeply personal and can vary from one individual to another. It might be a quiet corner of your home, a serene spot in nature, or any place that allows for reflection and uninterrupted dialogue with God. The key is finding a space that resonates with you personally, where you feel at ease to open your heart and mind to God's presence.

Integrating the "Secret Place" into Your Daily Life

Making the "Secret Place" part of your everyday routine is essential. It could be a few minutes at the start or end of the day or any moment you can dedicate to solitude and prayer. The duration is less significant than the quality and purpose of the time spent in this sacred space.

Overcoming Challenges

Creating and maintaining a "Secret Place" in the hustle and bustle of modern life can be challenging. To carve out time and space in our hectic lives, we must make a conscious effort. However, the spiritual advantages of having a dedicated space for prayer and thought are immense, providing a closer relationship with God as well as a more focused, tranquil life.

The Role of the "Secret Place" in Spiritual Growth

The "Secret Place" is not just about finding a physical location but about fostering a state of heart and mind where one can retreat to engage with God. It is about developing a rhythm of retreat and return, where solitude with God fuels our engagement with the world. This sacred space serves as a basis for spiritual growth, transforming prayer from a duty to a cherished refuge.

Self-Reflective Questions:

1. How can I enhance my morning routine to prioritize spiritual connection with Jesus?

----

2. What specific practices can I incorporate into my morning devotional time to set a spiritual tone for the day?

3. How can I deepen my moments of reflective prayer to better align my thoughts, decisions, and actions with His teachings?

4. How can I integrate Scripture meditation more effectively into my daily routine to shape my actions and decisions?

5. How can I improve my evening review process to cultivate a greater sense of gratitude, confession, and spiritual growth?

6. Am I actively participating in communal worship experiences to reinforce my daily spiritual routine?

7. How can I deepen my engagement with my faith community to provide and receive support, accountability, and fellowship?

8. How does my "Secret Place" contribute to my overall spiritual journey, and how can I personalize it further to enhance its effectiveness?

----

9. What strategies can I implement to overcome challenges and ensure regular, quality time for solitude and prayer?

Action Prompts:

- **Morning Devotion Enhancement:**
  Set specific goals for your morning devotional time, such as incorporating prayer, Scripture reading, and meditation, and commit to implementing them consistently.

- **Reflective Prayer Practices:**
  Create reminders or triggers throughout your day to pause and engage in reflective prayer, whether it's during transitions, moments of stress, or times of gratitude.

- **Scripture Meditation Plan:**
  Develop a structured approach to Scripture meditation, such as selecting a passage each day to study deeply, journaling about its application in your life, and sharing insights with others.

- **Evening Review Ritual:**
  Establish a nightly routine for your evening review, including journaling about your day, expressing gratitude, seeking forgiveness, and setting intentions for spiritual growth.

- **Community Worship Commitment:**
  Make a commitment to actively participate in weekly community worship experiences, such as attending church services, joining small groups, or engaging in online discussions.

- **"Secret Place" Establishment:**
  Designate a specific area in your home or surroundings as your "Secret Place" for prayer and reflection, personalizing it with meaningful items or decor that enhance your sense of connection with God.
- **Integrating Solitude into Daily Routine:**
  Schedule dedicated time slots in your daily routine for solitude and prayer, prioritizing these moments as essential for your spiritual well-being and growth.

Module 3: Becoming Like Him

Identifying Areas for Spiritual Formation

Identifying areas for spiritual development necessitates an understanding of the intricate interaction between our natural tendencies, the effect of our surroundings, and the life-changing power of engaging in spiritual disciplines demonstrated by Jesus. The pursuit of knowledge is crucial for anyone seeking to align their life more closely with Christ-like principles.

Recognizing Inherent Tendencies

Spiritual formation begins with accepting our innate inclinations, sometimes known as our "sin nature" in Christian theology. This encompasses not just our acts, but also our natural impulses and deep-seated habits that keep us from living a life consistent with Jesus' teachings. Understanding these inclinations is the first step toward identifying areas that demand modification.

Impact of Environment

Our environment has a huge impact on our spiritual development. This includes the stories we believe, our daily routines, and the company we keep. Each of these aspects may either guide us toward a life that reflects Jesus' teachings or lead us astray. Recognizing the effect of our surroundings allows us to recognize which elements of our lives require reformation in order to foster spiritual growth.

Engaging with Spiritual Disciplines

Spiritual formation is not solely about recognizing our shortcomings or the negative influences of our environment. It's about actively engaging with practices that Jesus modeled, such as prayer, meditation on Scripture, and communal living. These disciplines are not just activities but transformative practices that, when integrated into our daily lives, help reshape our desires, habits, and relationships towards a more Christ-centered existence.

The Role of Community

Spiritual formation relies heavily on community. It provides a support structure for accountability, encouragement, and collaborative progress. Engaging with a community of believers helps in recognizing personal areas of spiritual growth and provides a platform for applying Jesus' teachings in relational contexts.

Continuous Process

Identifying areas for spiritual formation is a continuous process, akin to an ongoing audit of one's life and practices. It demands a commitment to constant self-examination, an openness to change, and the humility to acknowledge areas for improvement. This process is not about attaining perfection, but about growing in our quest to become more like Jesus, accepting His teachings and embodying His love and grace in all aspects of our lives.

Developing a Personal Rule of Life

Creating a personal Rule of Life involves creating a structured approach to spiritual growth and discipleship that aligns with your innermost desires for transformation in Christ. This framework not only serves as a guide for your journey but also provides the necessary support for you to flourish in your relationship with God and in your daily living.

Understanding the Rule of Life

The concept of a Rule of Life originates from the early Christian tradition, where it served as a practical guide for individuals and communities to live out their faith intentionally. A Rule of Life encompasses a set of practices, relationships, and commitments that foster spiritual growth and alignment with God's will.

Components of a Rule of Life

1. **Spiritual Practices:** These are the fundamental actions that enable a profound and genuine connection with God. They might include prayer, Scripture reading, meditation, and other practices that improve your spiritual life.
2. **Relational Rhythms:** Our connections and interactions with others have a tremendous influence on our spiritual advancement. This includes community participation, accountability partnerships, and how we serve and love people around us.
3. **Commitments:** These are the promises or vows we make to uphold certain values or behaviors that are important to our spiritual journey. They reflect our dedication to following Christ and living out our faith in every aspect of our lives.

Creating Your Rule of Life

1. **Reflect on Your Desires:** Begin by contemplating your deepest desires for your relationship with God and your spiritual growth. Which aspects of Jesus' life and teachings do you feel compelled to embody more fully?
2. **Identify Practices and Rhythms:** Based on your reflection, identify specific spiritual practices and relational rhythms that resonate with your spiritual goals. Consider practices that help you connect with God and others.
3. **Set Clear Commitments:** Determine the commitments necessary to support your journey towards God. These

should represent your ideals and how you feel compelled to serve and interact with the world.

4. **Integrate into daily life:** Look for ways to incorporate your Rule of Life into your daily routines and schedules. It should be practical and adaptable, allowing for development and change as you progress in your spiritual journey.

Living Your Rule of Life

A Rule of Life is a dynamic framework that should change with you. Regularly examine and modify your Rule to suit your current spiritual needs and life situations. Remember, the objective is not to follow a precise set of rules, but to cultivate a life that is firmly anchored in Christ and reflects His love and grace.

Embrace the Journey

Embarking on this journey of developing and living out a personal Rule of Life is a transformative process. It invites you into a deeper relationship with God, nurtures your spiritual growth, and equips you to live out your faith in a way that is authentic and life-giving.

Self-Reflective Questions:

1. What are my innate inclinations and habits that may hinder my alignment with Christ-like principles?

----

2. How does my environment, including daily routines and social circles, influence my spiritual development?

3. Which aspects of my surroundings contribute positively to my spiritual growth, and which ones may need adjustment?

4. How does my involvement in a community of believers support my spiritual growth and accountability?

5. In what ways can I actively participate in community life to apply Jesus' teachings in relational contexts?

6. How can I maintain humility and acceptance of areas for improvement without striving for perfection?

7. What are my deepest desires for spiritual transformation and growth in Christ?

8. Which spiritual practices, relational rhythms, and commitments resonate most with my spiritual goals?

9. How can I integrate my Rule of Life into my daily routines and adapt it to suit my evolving spiritual needs?

10. What steps can I take to ensure that my Rule of Life remains dynamic and reflective of my ongoing spiritual journey?

Action Prompts:

- **Self-Reflection Exercise:**
  Dedicate time for introspection to identify and acknowledge inherent tendencies that may hinder spiritual growth.

- **Environment Evaluation:**
  Assess the influence of your environment on your spiritual development and identify areas for adjustment or improvement.

- **Discipline Integration Plan:**
  Create a structured plan to incorporate spiritual disciplines into your daily routine, setting specific goals for prayer, Scripture meditation, and communal engagement.

- **Community Engagement Strategy:**
  Actively seek opportunities for involvement in a community of believers, whether through church activities, small groups, or accountability partnerships.

- **Ongoing Self-Examination:**
  Establish a regular practice of self-reflection and assessment to maintain humility and openness to spiritual growth.

- **Rule of Life Development:**
  Reflect on your desires for spiritual transformation and use them as a foundation for developing a personal Rule of Life.

- **Integration and Adaptation:**
  Integrate your Rule of Life into your daily routines and regularly evaluate and adapt it to reflect your evolving spiritual journey.

Module 4: Doing as He Did

Practicing Hospitality as a Way of Life

Practicing hospitality as a way of life, according to "Practicing the Way", is an essential rhythm for making space for the gospel in our increasingly post-Christian culture. Hospitality, as exemplified by Jesus, is more than just sharing a meal; it is also about opening our lives and homes to others, particularly those who are marginalized or considered outsiders. This act of welcome provides an environment in which true connections can develop and God's transformational love can be experienced.

Hospitality in a Hostile World

Our contemporary cultural atmosphere is often apathetic, if not hostile, to the Christian message. However, Jesus demonstrated that hospitality—inviting others into our lives and homes—can overcome gaps and soften hearts. By sharing meals and life with others, as Jesus did with individuals like Zacchaeus, we exhibit a welcome attitude that may lead to meaningful conversations and connections.

The Power of Table Fellowship

In first-century Jewish society, eating a meal was a powerful symbol of inclusion and acceptance. Jesus used meals to bridge societal divides and convey God's invitation to the kingdom. He dined with individuals whom society had rejected, demonstrating that God's love knew no bounds. This practice of eating and drinking with others, particularly those who are far from God, is a potent form of hospitality that has the potential to transform lives.

Hospitality as Love in Action

The New Testament term for hospitality, "philoxenia," is derived from the Greek words for love ("philo") and stranger ("xenos"). This concept extends beyond simply welcoming visitors; it is about loving the stranger and turning them into a neighbor and, eventually, a member of God's family. By embracing hospitality, we reflect God's inclusive love and provide a space for others to experience Him.

Creating a Hospitable Space

Hospitality is more than just opening our doors; it is about sharing our emotions and lives with others. It takes intentionality to seek out folks who are lonely, disenfranchised, or in need of support. By providing a welcoming environment, we follow Jesus' example and allow life-changing connections to blossom.

The Role of Hospitality in Spiritual Formation

Integrating hospitality into our way of life is not just a good deed; it's a spiritual discipline that shapes us to be more like Jesus. As we welcome others, we learn to see them through God's eyes and love them with His love. This practice not only transforms those we welcome but also changes us, making us more compassionate, empathetic, and reflective of Christ's character.

Engaging in Service and Outreach

Engaging in service and outreach is fundamentally about embodying the ethos of Jesus Christ, who came not to be served, but to serve others. This approach to living is not just an activity but a profound transformation of how we view and interact with the world around us.

The essence of service

Jesus' life and teachings set a clear example for service. He demonstrated through actions, such as washing the feet of His disciples, that true leadership and discipleship involve serving others, even in the most menial tasks. This act was not only a demonstration of humility but also an invitation to his followers to live in a similar manner.

Healing Through Service

Service holds a transformative power not only for those being served but also for the server. Individuals who engage in acts of service confront their own egos, entitlements, and self-centeredness. The act of serving, particularly as Jesus did, blurs the distinction between the server and the served, benefiting both parties. The recipient's dignity is restored, and the giver is freed from self-absorption.

Service as a Daily Practice

Service is not confined to grand gestures or formal volunteerism alone; it is found in the everyday opportunities to assist, care for, and uplift others. Whether it's aiding a neighbor, parenting, or caring for aging family members, service is woven into the fabric of everyday life. Each act of service is a step toward following Jesus' example and giving our lives for the benefit of others.

Societal Impact

In a world rife with injustice, division, and inequality, service stands as a powerful antidote. It challenges societal norms of status and power dynamics, proposing a community where individuals look out for one another's needs. This approach has the potential to bridge divides and heal some of the deepest societal wounds.

Personal Transformation

Participating in service and outreach promotes personal growth. Service teaches people to see beyond their own needs and desires. This shift in perspective fosters a deeper sense of empathy, compassion, and connection to others. It's in the giving of ourselves that we find true fulfillment and understand the blessedness that Jesus spoke of.

Self-Reflective Questions:

1. How do I currently view and practice hospitality in my life, and what motivates me to do so?

2. In what ways can I deepen my understanding of hospitality as a transformative practice aligned with Jesus' example?

3. Am I intentional about welcoming others into my life and home, especially those who may be marginalized or considered outsiders?

4. How can I overcome any barriers or hesitations I may have in opening up my life and space to others?

5. Do I actively seek to turn strangers into neighbors through acts of love and hospitality?

6. How can I cultivate an environment of hospitality beyond simply opening my doors, to genuinely sharing my emotions and life with others?

7. What steps can I take to make my space more welcoming and conducive to meaningful connections?

----

8. In what ways has practicing hospitality shaped my spiritual growth and character?

----

9. How can I further integrate hospitality into my spiritual discipline to become more compassionate, empathetic, and Christ-like?

10. How has engaging in acts of service impacted my own personal growth and perspective?

11. What areas of self-centeredness or entitlement do I need to confront and address through continued acts of service?

Action Prompts:

- **Hospitality Assessment:**
  Reflect on your current hospitality practices and motivations, and identify areas where you can deepen your understanding and engagement.

- **Intentional Welcoming:**
  Set a goal to intentionally welcome others into your life and home, particularly those who may feel marginalized or excluded.

- **Love in Action:**
  Plan and execute acts of love and acceptance towards strangers, seeking to turn them into neighbors and ultimately members of God's family.

- **Creating Welcoming Spaces:**
  Take practical steps to create a hospitable environment in your home and life, including sharing your emotions and life with others authentically.

- **Integration into Spiritual Discipline:**
  Integrate hospitality into your spiritual discipline by incorporating intentional acts of hospitality into your daily routine and prayer life.

- **Service Engagement Plan:**
  Develop a plan for engaging in acts of service and outreach in your community, ensuring your motivations are aligned with Jesus' example of selfless love.

- **Personal Transformation Focus:**
  Reflect on areas of personal growth and transformation through acts of service, and set goals to address any remaining barriers to selflessness and humility.

Module 5: Cultivating a Rule of Life

Building Your Own Rule of Life

Building Your Own Rule of Life, outlined in Comer's book, involves setting up a personalized framework for spiritual growth by integrating certain practices, relationships, and commitments into your daily life. This concept, deeply rooted in the ancient traditions of the church, is designed to create space for an individual to be with Jesus, become like Him, and do as He did.

Understanding the Rule of Life

A Rule of Life is not about imposing a set of rigid regulations upon oneself but rather about establishing a life-giving structure that supports spiritual formation. The term originates from the Latin word "regula," which can refer to a trellis in a vineyard. Just as a trellis supports a vine, enabling it to grow upwards and bear fruit, a Rule of Life provides the necessary support for spiritual growth, directing us towards God and allowing us to flourish.

Components of a Rule of Life

A Rule of Life consists of a schedule, practices, and relational rhythms that are in tune with one's deepest desire to live in communion with God. It is a deliberate structuring of one's life around the most crucial aspect: the relationship with God. This rule is inspired by the Holy Spirit and aims at fostering wholeness in Christ, making it a dynamic and evolving framework rather than a static set of rules.

Purpose of a Rule of Life

The primary goal of a Rule of Life is to provide a structure that facilitates an intimate and growing relationship with Jesus. It is about making intentional decisions about integrating spiritual disciplines into your life, including prayer, Scripture reading, Sabbath observance, and community involvement, in a way that nurtures your soul and allows you to exemplify Christ's love and teachings in your daily deeds.

Crafting Your Rule of Life

1. **Identify your deepest desires:** Consider what you most genuinely desire in your connection with God and how you wish to grow spiritually.
2. **Choose Your Practices:** Select spiritual disciplines and practices that resonate with your spiritual journey and will help you grow closer to Jesus. Consider practices that foster both personal intimacy with God and engagement with your community.
3. **Set Relational Rhythms:** Define how you will engage with the people in your life, including your faith community, family, and others, to practice the love and hospitality Jesus modeled.
4. **Create a schedule:** Designate specific times for your chosen practices and relational engagements, ensuring they are integrated into the rhythm of your daily life.

Living Your Rule of Life

Implementing your Rule of Life involves dedication and adaptability. It is a living document that should be revisited and adjusted as you grow and your circumstances change. The aim is not to adhere to a rigid set of behaviors but to use your Rule of Life as a guide that keeps you anchored to your core values and spiritual goals, even when "love falters."

Integrating the Rule into Daily Life

Integrating the Rule of Life into daily living requires following a systematic approach to spiritual growth, inspired by ancient church practices and profoundly anchored in Jesus' teachings. This framework, known as the Rule of Life, is not about rigid adherence to a set of rules but about creating a supportive structure, much like a trellis for a vine, that enables us to grow towards God and bear spiritual fruit.

Embracing the Rule of Life

The Rule of Life consists of a schedule, practices, and relational rhythms designed to create space for being with Jesus, becoming like Him, and doing as He did. This involves organizing our lives around spiritual disciplines that align with our deepest desires to live in communion with God. Rich Villodas articulates this concept as a set of practices, relationships, and commitments inspired by the Spirit for the sake of our wholeness in Christ.

The Trellis Metaphor

The metaphor of a trellis in a vineyard illustrates the function of the Rule of Life beautifully. Just as a trellis supports a vine to grow upward and bear fruit by providing structure, the Rule of Life supports our spiritual growth by providing a framework that guides our growth in the desired direction. Without this enabling structure, our spiritual life may be stunted or become vulnerable to different challenges.

To integrate the Rule of Life into daily living, consider the following steps:

1. **Define Your Practices:** Determine which spiritual disciplines resonate with you and will help you grow closer to Jesus. These might include prayer, Scripture reading, Sabbath observance, and engaging in community activities.

2. **Set a schedule:** Integrate these practices into your daily and weekly routines. Allocate specific times for prayer, meditation, community involvement, and rest, ensuring these activities are woven into the fabric of your day.
3. **Embrace Relational Rhythms:** Establish rhythms of relationship that reflect the love and hospitality of Jesus. This could involve regular gatherings with a faith community, mentoring relationships, and hospitality within your home.
4. **Stay Flexible:** The Rule of Life should give structure while also allowing for flexibility. Life's circumstances change, and our spiritual practices need to adapt accordingly. The Rule is a living document that should be revisited and adjusted as needed.
5. **Seek Guidance:** Engage with a spiritual director, mentor, or faith community to discuss your Rule of Life. External input might bring helpful insights and support to keep you on track with your spiritual aspirations.
6. **Reflect and Adjust:** Regularly reflect on the effectiveness of your Rule of Life. Is it bringing you closer to God? Are you becoming more like Jesus in character and action? Make changes as needed to ensure that your Rule is in sync with your spiritual path.

Integrating the Rule of Life into daily living is about more than just adopting a set of spiritual practices; it's about orienting your entire life around the goal of deepening your relationship with Jesus. This deliberate framework fosters your spiritual development, controls your behaviors, and enables you to live out your faith in a way that is genuine and transformative.

Self-Reflective Questions:

1. What are my deepest desires regarding my relationship with God, and how do I envision my spiritual growth unfolding?

----

2. Which spiritual disciplines resonate with me the most, and how can I incorporate them into my daily life to draw closer to Jesus?

----

3. How do I engage with others in my life, and how can I cultivate relationships that reflect Jesus' love and hospitality?

---

4. Am I willing to commit to a structured framework for spiritual growth, even if it requires adjustments and sacrifices?

---

5. How flexible am I in adapting my spiritual practices and commitments to changing life circumstances and seasons?

---

6. What evidence of spiritual growth and transformation do I observe in my life as I engage with my Rule of Life?

---

7. Are my daily actions and behaviors aligned with the core values and spiritual goals outlined in my Rule of Life?

Action Prompts:

- **Identifying Spiritual Desires:**
  Dedicate time for introspection and journaling to clarify your deepest desires and aspirations for spiritual growth.

- **Selecting Meaningful Practices:**
  Research various spiritual disciplines and choose a few that resonate with you deeply, considering how they can be integrated into your daily routine.

- **Nurturing Relationships:**
  Plan intentional gatherings or activities with friends, family, or your faith community to cultivate deeper relationships grounded in love and hospitality.

- **Committing to Growth:**
  Make a commitment to prioritize your spiritual growth by setting aside specific times each day for prayer, meditation, and reflection.

- **Embracing Flexibility:**
  Embrace the concept of flexibility by acknowledging that life is dynamic, and adjustments to your Rule of Life may be necessary over time.

- **Regular Reflection:**
  Schedule regular times for reflection on your spiritual journey, evaluating the effectiveness of your practices and making adjustments as needed.

- **Seeking Support and Guidance:**
  Reach out to a spiritual mentor, counselor, or trusted friend to discuss your Rule of Life and gain insights or encouragement for your journey.

Module 6: Embracing the Cross

Understanding Surrender and Sacrifice

"Understanding Surrender and Sacrifice" entails acknowledging the profound commitment required to follow Jesus, which is ultimately about relinquishing one's own desires, aspirations, and even life as we know it in order to embark on a journey of deep change and alignment with God's purpose.

The High Bar of Entry

Following Jesus is not a casual decision; it involves a high bar of entry that demands everything from an individual. This sacrifice is not a one-time act, but rather a continuous practice of denying oneself, accepting one's cross, and genuinely embodying the essence of discipleship. It is about making the intentional decision to forgo one's own path in favor of Jesus'.

Symbol of the Cross

The cross, an emblem of suffering and sacrifice, symbolizes the ultimate surrender and sacrifice—death to self. This concept, though metaphorical for many today, carries the weight of a literal reality for the early disciples, many of whom faced martyrdom because of their unwavering commitment to Jesus. Their sacrifices underline the severity of following Jesus, pointing out that while discipleship may not result in physical death in contemporary contexts, it does involve the death of self-will and ego.

Surrender as the Foundation

Surrender is foundational to spiritual life and discipleship. It's described as a lifelong process of deepening one's surrender to Jesus, where love for God and surrender to His will become indistinguishable. This submission is not passive, but rather a conscious and purposeful decision to align one's will with God's, even if it goes against personal inclinations or societal norms.

Obedience and willingness

In this process, surrender is inextricably linked to obedience. True discipleship is distinguished by an unshakeable commitment to following Jesus' teachings, recognizing that such devotion is not a burden, but rather a liberation from the self-centeredness that ensnares. The greatest expression of human will, in this context, is not exerting one's desires but yielding to God's direction and guidance.

The paradox of surrender

The paradox of Christian discipleship is rooted in the principle that by dying to oneself, one truly finds life. This surrender, while countercultural in a society that values self-actualization, is the pathway to realizing one's true self and fulfilling one's deepest heart desires. Jesus, the essence of submission, exhibits this in His prayer at Gethsemane, when He prioritizes the Father's will before His own.

Committing to a Life of Discipleship

Committing to a life of discipleship, as explained in "Practicing the Way," is an invitation to begin a transformative journey under Jesus' leadership, using His teachings, practices, and manner of life as a pattern for our own. This journey is more than just accepting a set of ideas; it is about enduring a fundamental transformation that aligns our life with the ideals and principles exhibited by Jesus.

The Call to Apprenticeship

Dallas Willard, a renowned philosopher, famously stated that there is no problem in human life that apprenticeship to Jesus cannot solve. This notion demonstrates the comprehensive impact of discipleship on an individual's life, addressing issues from personal struggles to broader societal challenges. Discipleship to Jesus provides a way of life that addresses the human condition, such as political conflict, climate change, mental health issues, and more.

Understanding The Commitment

Jesus' invitation to "Come follow me" is a call to a deep, intentional commitment that goes beyond mere conversion or church attendance. It is an invitation to apprentice under Him, to adopt His way of living as our own. This commitment involves counting the cost and understanding what we are saying "yes" to—a life that is radically different from the norm, centered on Jesus' teachings and example.

Transformation Through Discipleship

The promise of transformation is central to the discipleship process. By arranging our lives around the practices, rhythms, and truths that Jesus Himself embodied, we open ourselves to God's power to change us from the inside out. This change is not spontaneous; it involves a deliberate effort to follow Jesus' example and learn from Him how to live in conformity with God's kingdom.

Practicing the Way

True discipleship means practicing "the Way" of Jesus, integrating His teachings into every aspect of our lives. This involves more than just intellectual assent to a set of doctrines; it's about living out those teachings daily, allowing them to shape our actions, decisions, and interactions with others. It's a journey of becoming more like Jesus, reflecting His love, grace, and truth in our own lives.

The Outcome of Discipleship

The ultimate goal of committing to a life of discipleship is to become the people we were meant to be, living the lives we were destined for. This does not imply reaching a point of perfection, but rather growing in our relationship with Jesus and becoming more aligned with His character and teachings. It is about discovering our actual identity and purpose in Him and living it out in the world.

Self-Reflective Questions:

1. Am I willing to embrace the high bar of entry to follow Jesus, which demands continuous sacrifice and surrender of my desires?

----

2. What does surrender mean to me, and how deeply am I willing to align my will with God's, even if it contradicts my personal inclinations?

----

3. How do I perceive obedience in the context of discipleship, and am I willing to prioritize following Jesus' teachings above my own desires?

4. Do I grasp the paradoxical nature of surrender, understanding that by yielding to God's will, I ultimately find true life and fulfillment?

---

5. Am I ready to commit to a transformative journey of discipleship under Jesus' leadership, understanding the profound impact it will have on every aspect of my life?

---

6. Have I counted the cost of discipleship, comprehending the radical difference it entails from societal norms and being prepared for the commitment it requires?

---

7. How do I envision my growth and transformation through discipleship, and what steps am I willing to take to align my life more closely with Jesus' teachings?

8. What areas of my life am I reluctant to surrender or sacrifice to follow Jesus, and what underlying reasons contribute to this resistance?

---

9. How do I measure my spiritual growth and progress in discipleship, and what indicators suggest that I am aligning more closely with Jesus' teachings and example?

Action Prompts:

- **Daily Surrender Practice:**
  Start each day with a prayer of surrender, consciously relinquishing your desires and aligning your will with God's.

- **Regular Self-Examination:**
  Set aside time weekly for self-reflection and examination of your obedience to Jesus' teachings, identifying areas for improvement and growth.

- **Intentional Sacrificial Acts:**
  Incorporate intentional acts of sacrifice into your routine, such as serving others sacrificially or giving up personal comforts for the sake of someone in need.

- **Joining a Discipleship Group:**
  Seek out a discipleship group or accountability partner where you can discuss your journey, receive support, and grow together in following Jesus.

- **Scripture Meditation Practice:**
  Dedicate regular time for deep meditation on Scripture, focusing on passages that emphasize surrender, sacrifice, and discipleship.

- **Service and Outreach Engagement:**
  Engage in service and outreach activities in your community, actively demonstrating Jesus' love and compassion to those in need.

- **Practicing the Way Daily:**
  Commit to living out Jesus' teachings daily in practical ways, whether it's through acts of kindness, forgiveness, or seeking reconciliation in relationships.

Conclusion

Bringing It All Together

Committing to a life of discipleship is an invitation to embark on a redefining journey with Jesus, using His teachings, practices, and manner of life as a model for your own. This journey is about undergoing a profound change that aligns our lives with the values and principles exemplified by Jesus.

The Call to Apprenticeship

Dallas Willard, a renowned philosopher, famously stated that there is no problem in human life that apprenticeship to Jesus cannot solve. This concept emphasizes the broad influence of discipleship on a person's life, covering anything from private issues to broader societal issues. Discipleship to Jesus provides a way of life that addresses the human condition, such as political conflict, climate change, mental health difficulties, and more.

Understanding The Commitment

Jesus' invitation to "Come follow me" is a call to an intentional, purposeful commitment that transcends beyond conversion and church attendance. It is an invitation to apprentice under Him, to adopt His way of living as our own. This commitment involves counting the cost and understanding what we are saying "yes" to—a life that is radically different from the norm, centered on Jesus' teachings and example.

Transformation Through Discipleship

The heart of discipleship lies in the promise of transformation. By arranging our lives around the practices, rhythms, and truths that Jesus Himself embodied, we open ourselves to God's power to change us from the inside out. This transformation is not automatic; it requires a deliberate effort to follow Jesus' way, learning from Him how to live in accordance with God's kingdom.

Practicing the Way

True discipleship is following "the Way" of Jesus and incorporating His teachings into all aspects of your life. This involves living out those teachings daily, allowing them to shape our actions, decisions, and interactions with others. It's a journey of becoming more like Jesus, reflecting His love, grace, and truth in our own lives.

The Outcome of Discipleship

The ultimate goal of committing to a life of discipleship is to become the people we were meant to be, living the lives we were destined for. This doesn't mean achieving a state of perfection but rather growing continuously in our relationship with Jesus and becoming more aligned with His character and teachings. It's about finding our true identity and purpose in Him and living out that reality in the world.

Next Steps on Your Journey

As we reach the conclusion of this journey, it's critical to reflect on the transformative path of discipleship we've taken and evaluate the next phase in our spiritual journey. The teachings and principles laid out in this workbook are practical tools designed to be lived out daily, fostering a deeper relationship with Jesus and a more Christ-like life.

Deepening your commitment

The journey doesn't end here; it's an ongoing process of deepening your commitment to living as Jesus lived. This involves continuously seeking to understand His teachings more profoundly and applying them more faithfully in every aspect of life. It's about making a conscious effort to remain connected to the vine, drawing sustenance and strength from Jesus to bear fruit in every season.

Integrating Practices into Daily Life

The practices and disciplines discussed in this workbook are meant to be woven into the fabric of your daily routine. Prayer, meditation, service to others, and hospitality are all ways to exemplify Jesus' love, grace, and truth. Evaluate your current routines and consider where these practices can be more fully integrated to transform your everyday life

Engaging in Community

Discipleship is not a solitary journey. It thrives in the context of community where believers can support, encourage, and challenge one another. Seek out a community of like-minded individuals committed to "Practicing the Way." Participate in frequent fellowship, accountability, and communal worship to develop your faith and grow together in the image of Christ.

Embracing Continuous Learning

The path of discipleship is one of lifelong learning. There is always more to learn about God, His Word, and how to live your faith in a changing world. Commit to being a perpetual student of the Scriptures and the teachings of Jesus. Attend courses, workshops, and conferences to broaden your knowledge and practice of discipleship.

Serving and Outreach

Discipleship inevitably leads to service and outreach. Look for ways to benefit your neighborhood and beyond. Consider how your unique gifts and passions can contribute to the needs around you and reflect the love of Jesus in tangible ways. Outreach is an expression of the overflow of God's love in your life, inviting others to experience the transformative power of the gospel.

Reflecting and adjusting

Regularly take time to reflect on your journey of discipleship. Assess areas of growth and identify aspects of your life that may require further surrender to Jesus. Be open to the Holy Spirit's guidance and be willing to adjust your practices, relationships, and commitments as you grow in your faith.

Moving Forward

As you continue on your journey, remember that discipleship is marked by both victories and challenges. There will be moments of profound joy and seasons of difficult growth. Through it all, keep your eyes fixed on Jesus, the perfecter of our faith, who invites us on this lifelong journey of transformation.

Final Notes & Reflections

Final Notes & Reflections

Final Notes & Reflections

Made in United States
Troutdale, OR
02/25/2024

17914622R00046